SELFDOM
The Essence of Oneself

by Dr. Leah M. Kelley

Blue Forge Press
Port Orchard, Washington

Selfdom: The Essence of Oneself
Copyright 2020
by Dr. Leah M. Kelley

First eBook Edition
April 2021

First Print Edition
April 2021

ISBN 978-1-59092-980-3

Cover art by Alex Powell

All rights reserved, including the right to reproduce this book or portions thereof in any form whatsoever, except in the case of short excerpts for use in reviews of the book.

For information about film, reprint or other subsidiary rights, contact blueforgegroup@gmail.com

This is a work of fiction. Names, characters, locations, and all other story elements are the product of the authors' imaginations and are used fictitiously. Any resemblance to actual persons, living or dead, or other elements in real life, is purely coincidental.

Blue Forge Press is the print division of the volunteer-run, federal 501(c)3 nonprofit company, Blue Forge Group, founded in 1989 and dedicated to bringing light to the shadows and voice to the silence. We strive to empower storytellers across all walks of life with our four divisions: Blue Forge Press, Blue Forge Films, Blue Forge Gaming, and Blue Forge Records. Find out more at www.BlueForgeGroup.org

Blue Forge Press
7419 Ebbert Drive Southeast
Port Orchard, Washington 98367
blueforgepress@gmail.com
360-550-2071 ph.txt

This book is dedicated to the giver of my gift (Jesus Christ), who gave me the talent, and ability, to bring words to life.

I would also like to dedicate this book to my entire family—I don't want to leave anyone out. I can't forget to mention my best friend, and ace boom cool, Geraldine A. Bowers. Thanks for being the friend many people desire, but few find. To my mom: Here it is, honey; and a special dedication to my siblings, children, and grandchildren. I love you all with an eternal love, believe me, and trust God, the best is yet to come. Also, thanks to Jennifer DiMarco, who gave me this opportunity to share my gift with the world.

Words can either bring life or death; there is power in words. Writing poetry is a therapeutic outlet for me, as I release my creativity, putting pen to paper, it allows me to bring my thoughts to life. This book was birthed out of the desire, to touch someone's life through the medium of poetry.

Follow your dreams, the impossible is possible. For you see I'm living it now, walking in the realm of possibilities.

Dr. Leah M. Kelley

Table of Contents

Selfdom	11
Walls	12
Into Me	13
You	15
Motionless	16
Breathe	18
This is New to Me	19
Vibration	20
Queen	21
Addiction	22
Rebirth	23
Taboo	24
Lovers & Lies	25
Screams	26
Mane	27
The Cup	28
Backslider	29
Acceptance	30
What I	31
Right is Right	33
I Gave My All	34
At First	35
Re-Group	36

Warrior	*38*
Lifeline	*39*
Out the Box	*40*
Bond	*41*
My Thoughts	*42*
You Chose	*43*
The Dark	*44*
I Can't Believe This	*45*
The World as I Knew It	*46*
Don't Go	*47*
Denial	*48*
Put it to an End	*49*
Words	*50*
Promises	*51*
Lies	*52*
Us	*53*
Come Away	*54*
The Ocean	*55*
View	*56*
Cold	*57*
Friendship	*58*
Attraction	*59*
Belief	*60*
Prison	*61*
Tell Me	*62*
Off	*63*
How Can You Love Us Both	*64*

Retake	65
Climb Higher	66
Tell Me Again	67
Courage	68
Temptation	69
Love	70
Within	71
It's Not Okay	72
Sorry	73
I'm Done	74
Jump	75
Why	76
No More	77
River	78
Treason	79
Sin	80
Slowdown	81
Puppet	82
Race	83
The Track	84
Encounter	85
Rebellion	86
Help	87
Voice	88
Vision	89
Not My Problem	90
Guilt	91

Regret	*92*
Bosom	*93*
Cycles	*94*
Remarkable	*95*
Subtitles	*96*
Soul Searching	*97*
Value	*98*
Past	*99*
Finally	*100*
Talents	*101*
About the Author	*102*

SELFDOM
The Essence of Oneself

by Dr. Leah M. Kelley

Selfdom

Rare, not easily attained

A once in a lifetime

Experience

Not often do you

Run into a woman of my character

Who knows their worth

And embraces their individuality

I know my identity

I am not defined

By the mere opinions of man

I was created for a greater purpose

And destiny

Committed

As I adhere to the plan

WALLS

I built walls around my heart, barbwire, and fire
Protecting it from future pain, lies, deceit, and the games
Walls that no one could penetrate, climb over, or get through
So, I thought, then comes you
With fire extinguishers, and wire cutters
The scars of the past remain
I was not looking for love, yet love had another plan
Now here you and I stand, face to face
With nowhere to run, there's choices to make
There are steps to take, toward the unknown
I swore love was my enemy, as you immediately assured me
You are not here to hurt me
But to help me forgive what was, and to accept what is
I cannot believe what's happening, am I dreaming?
Then suddenly… I am caught off guard by a
Gentle caress, my body responds
As you lay me down, I become putty in your hands
I open to receive your love, as I take a deep breath
Walls come crashing down, and my heart says yes
Pull me closer, as you go deeper
An embrace so intense our souls connect
As walls evaporate

Into Me

I had to look deep within, with a magnifying glass
Deeper than I wanted to go, the roots run deep
Did a little soul searching, got reacquainted with me
Was I afraid of what I would discover, possibly?
We as humans tend to allow denial,
To shield us from the truth
As bitter seeds are planted, taking root
We treat the truth as a foe, and a lie as our closest friend
I came to the realization, I was self-destructing
Bad relationships and more
Can I just be truthful right now?
I had to put an end to every destructive pattern
Re-think my choices, and reboot
I know someone reading this right now
Can relate
This is not on some crazy tip
But honestly when was the last time
You had a real heart to heart with you?
Before we make sure others are okay,
Our priority should be us
Into me I looked
And what I discovered

Was a masterpiece
Loved by the highest, redeemed
A walking testimony
What was designed to kill me
Only made me stronger
Now I walk the walk of champions
Free

You

You are already a permanent fixture
Cemented in my life
An unmovable presence
You light up every darkened area
Healing every broken place
Restoring hope, and my faith in love
My heart though butchered
You have managed to gather the pieces
Nurturing my bleeding heart, speaking life
Your love was the medicine I needed
Your kiss restored affection, started passions fire burning
Once again, honestly
Thought love was my enemy
Your actions assured me it was not my foe
Revealing to me the mysteries of love I never knew existed
You are my eternal love
My forever desire
I am your willing captive for evermore
You alone have changed my life

Motionless

Standing still, paralyzed in my tracks, motionless
Is this really happening?
As tears stream down my face,
time ceases, and shock takes over
All mental functions have ceased to function
Say it is not so, you are not really gone, this is a weird prank
A joke that I would not wish on my enemy
This rage and anger
A tug of war within me
I miss you more than mere words can utter
Nothing can define my pain, for it is indescribable
It's not the same here without you
Even though we put on a face as if it is
The mask that we hide behind is grief
Our hearts are broken, desperately needing repair
If only I can hear your voice, kneel with you in prayer
Feel the love in your embrace, open my eyes and you are there
I never knew missing you would be such an unbearable weight
The memory of you give me strength
Your laughter penetrates eternity
Heard through the portals of time
Serenading me from a distance, soothing the pain

It plays over and over in my head
like beautifully written love song
How did everything go left?
How did everything go wrong?

I smelled your favorite flower today
I was intoxicated by its fragrance
Thoughts of you hold my thoughts captive
I think of you every holiday
Your birthday is the hardest for me
The world is celebrating it with firecrackers and declarations
My world came crashing when you transcended
I miss you, and every day I am reminded
Of what you imparted in me
And I will forever be grateful, Grandma

Breathe

You are my oxygen, my life source
I will suffocate without you
Gasping for my next breath
Longing for your mouth to mouth resuscitation
I am fighting to regain my composure
Lost in the dark
No light in sight
This is a fight for my life, you are the love of my life
The fire of jealousy that was ignited
I saw you with them
What was your plight
Me vs them
Us intertwined
The plot that was devised in secret
The repeated knives in my back
My naivety did not prepare me for the attack
I trusted those that did not deserve my loyalty
Was this due to my emotional frailty?

This is New to Me

I never felt like this before
I have a new pep in my step
Little more glow to my face
The butterflies have not ceased to flutter
Word to my mother
This feels good
I don't ever want this feeling to flee
It is just you and me
I have never been swept off my feet
You entered my world
And turned it completely upside down
Loving me like I have never been loved before
My track record with love has not been the best
Since you have entered my life, I've forgotten about
Those before you, they no longer matter
They no longer exist
You put the pieces of my heart back together
Clearing up all the emotional clutter
This is all new to me
Your love caught me off guard
I was not expecting it to be you
But I am glad it is you

Vibration

You are a powerful vibration
A movement of your own
Lost in a zone
Of euphoria
When you touch me
My entire body shakes
Inner quakes
Sending waves of ecstasy
Throughout
From my head to my toes
It generates orgasmic pleasure
Bringing me to heights
Of climactic depths

Queen

You're still beautiful
Do not focus on your scars
Stop pointing out your flaws
We all make mistakes
Experiencing regret is human
Forgive yourself
Free yourself from that mental cage
We all get wiser with age
You're beautiful
Let go of that low self-esteem
And fix your crown
Queen

Addiction

I tried to fight it
Even denied it
Said it was not so
Hid it from everyone
Took every precaution
To avoid it
Yet I fell prey to it
Your love is so contagious
It has become my addiction
I will do anything
In order to get it
Withdrawals if I go a day without
Experiencing it
I got it bad
Real bad
My heart skips a beat
By the mere thought of what
Your love does to me
So, tell me, when will I?
Get another hit?

Rebirth

What a breath of fresh air, felt like I was suffocating

I am free as a bird, a rebirth has taken place

A weight has been lifted off my shoulders

I am free, free indeed to spread my wings

And soar with eagles

Thank you, lord, you heard my cry

Giving an ear to my prayer

I trust you with everything

For you know what is best for me

You never take something away

Without replacing it with something better

My turn is coming, my blessing is on its way

The enemy tried to destroy me

But you protected me, and guarded my heart

And restored me

Taboo

Keep it a secret
It must stay hidden
The abuse, molestation, the rape of the innocent
Never to be mentioned
Sweep it under the rug
Deny it ever happened
You better not tell a soul
It was your daddy, aunty, Uncle Bo
As old ladies, sit on porches
Gossiping like hens
Dipping snuff
Acting as though
The world they live in is sinless
Mother Sue
Aunt Mable
And Mrs.-Know-It-All
They always had the inside intel
But would never tell
For it was taboo to talk about it
As tears flow like rivers
And bellies swell

Lovers & Lies

Betrayal, vows broken
Lovers lay in marital beds
Union defiled
Secrets and manipulation
Playing mind games
Man, this is one awkward situation
Adultery becomes commonplace
Sin has replaced ethics
Ones character is now on trial
Reasoning has fled
The flesh has now taking over
The heart has shifted, waxing cold
The wife has been replaced
And now the mistress receives the love
Intended for the wife
Harbored anger, manifested strife
the war has now begun
wrestling between what is wrong
from what is right
lovers & lies
no longer can you hide

Screams

Screams of pain
Echoed from within
I will never be able to wash this off with soap
While my body lay fragile
Battered, broken, and bruised
Comfortless nights
Tears that burn like acid
Scars remain
I put the darkness in the back of my mind
The memories soon fade
Suppressed emotion
Resentment takes the helm
While lies seal the deal
The fake vs the real
The rent still is paid
From the back of my sacrifice
And my mother
None the wiser
As she continues to be deceived
By the man who claims to love her

Mane

Mane I swear you the realest
Naw I'm serious
I ain't never met a man like you
You always keep it a hundred
Is you real, or are you bullcornin?
Come on mane you can tell me
I am your girl
Your secret is safe with me
Why you looking at me like that?
Acting like you ain't heard nobody
No problem
Well, remember that next time
You need something

The Cup

I am drunk off loves liquor
Intoxicated
Absolutely hammered
Staggering
Walking around with
My head in the clouds
High off its
Spirits
I don't wanna come down
Unable to walk a straight line
Your love got me gone
And I don't wanna sober up
I love this feeling
It's like no other
You are the liquor of my choice

Backslider

I turned my back on what I knew was right
Willingly, I rebelled
I gave into the lust of my flesh
I saw what I wanted
And I went after it
Without a second thought
I had to have it
I craved it
Longed for it
No matter the cost
I was caught up in the trap
Of what it offered
For sin last only for a season
And unrepented sin leads to
A definite punishment
I had to come to myself
Just like the prodigal son
And return to my father's house
And repent

Acceptance

We seek acceptance from people who
Could care less, stop being men pleasers
Have you noticed?
We jump through hoops, with gasoline trousers
Trying to please them
And no matter what we do, they still won't accept us
We got to stop going out our way
For people who won't even cross
The street for us
And live our live to the fullest
Nonstop, fulfilling our dreams
And goals, as we allow success
To speak for itself

What I

What I feel for you is real
I cannot lie, though you wear a mask
I cannot deny what is true
And that is my feelings for you
I stand before you opened, and exposed
I refuse to hide
No matter the cost I will not lie
I carry in my heart every day the love I have for only you
However, there is another in this scenario
Who is clueless that your heart is divided
There are traces of me all over you
Connected are our souls
Knitted together
Woven for a lifetime
You are my love song
Playing continually, wooing me
I am yours, I vow this to you
And completely you are mine
My mind is consumed with thoughts of only you
I'm caught up in a whirlwind of love
Your love got me stuck, love struck
Mesmerized, honestly, I am hooked

And it only took one kiss
I fully surrender, can you handle this
We are fighting to be together
No matter the risk
Backs up against the wall
As the odds are stacked

Right is Right

You can't ignore it
Though you may try
You cannot think it away
Your actions speak louder than words
You are blind if you believe
That any negative behavior is acceptable
Right is right
And wrong is wrong
One must discipline themselves
To do the latter
If you do not
Correct the destructive patterns
In your life
It may eventually lead
To your own demise
In one way or the other

I Gave My All

I am so sick and tired
Of giving my all and getting nothing in return
It's beginning on wearing on me something heavy
Sleepless nights
Crying just out the blue
Screaming out loud for the respect that is overdue
The recognition that never seems to come
Trying to impress people that aren't worth impressing
I've come to realize
I refuse to dance by the beat of their drum
I'm a rebel
I must chart my own course
I gave my all, and yet my all wasn't good enough
I've come, to the conclusion
I'm done trying to please people
I'm focusing on me

At First

First it started out mentally

Then emotionally, and when you saw your plan was working

To break me down

The abuse graduated to physical

The emotional, and mental scars though brutal

At least I could hide them

But the black eyes, busted lips, and bruised arms

Was becoming more difficult, and harder to disguise

The pain was so intense, the turmoil unexplainable

I had no more tears left to cry

You lacked empathy

Your love for me never existed

How could you profess to love some one

And treat them so inhumane

I figured it out, all this was about control

A sick game

You were a counterfeit

Sent to destroy me

I recognize now your lies was used as bait

To woo me

Re-Group

Take a moment to get yourself together
Do not rush the process
Reconditioning your mind
From all the brainwashing
Will take time
You've been locked in a cage
Treated as an animal
Stripped of all that is rational
Forced to perform acts, losing control
Allow yourself time to regroup
Life I know, has dealt you a pretty ugly hand
Kidnapped, trafficked, in the wrong hands
Finally, you found a way out, never looking back
Despite the circumstances, you bounce back
Game is strong, many planned your untimely demise
Unmarked graves, easily disposed lives
I want to take the time to commend you
You fought the good fight, refusing to die
Not many have the testimony of survival
Jane doe's, lost identities, forgotten face, hearts bleed
What you been through, the storm, and the rain
A tsunami of pain

Would have destroyed anyone else
With a weakened will
The saying goes try to walk a mile in my shoes
You wouldn't be able to bear the cross
No one can tell your story like you can
Outlining ever detail of your escape
Victorious you stand

Warrior

I was conceived a child of rape, womb tainted
One of hate, not love
So, the story goes, only the two parties know
Flip a coin what are the odds knowing
That you were unwanted was a hard pill
To swallow, fatherless, nameless shaking my head
Heads or tails, is a snitch in the midst, that will reveal the details
Revealing the truth, come clean for once
Years to go by, and the identity is still a mystery
How can you live with such a secret knowing it's hurting me
There was a bounty on my head from the womb
Where life begins, and death passes over
I was sent here on assignment
Though this world is cruel
I was labeled as a misfit, and a bastard
As his blood roamed through my veins
Above that my purpose is bigger than
The shame
I let go of the pain
I regain my stance against adversity
And fight, I was anointed, and appointed
A warrior in the womb

LIFELINE

You threw me a lifeline
You saw me drowning
Rescuing me from
Myself
I will forever be grateful
I'm indebted to you
Thanks to you I have a second chance
To live the life
I was destined to live
Because of your lifeline

Out the Box

You got to think out the box
Challenge yourself
Stop standing in your own way
Remove the stumbling blocks
You're your biggest critic
Just to hard on yourself at times
Give yourself space to grow
Everyone makes mistakes
We are human
And we learn by trial and error
You have what it takes, it's in you
All things are possible if you just believe
You just need to cultivate it
And perfect it
Don't be afraid to enlarge your territory
Expand your knowledge, stretch yourself
Share your gift with the world
They're waiting
On you

Bond

Our bond was supposed to be thicker than water
No one, and I mean no one was supposed to be able
To penetrate it
We vowed to love no matter what
And to have each other's backs, whenever, and however
The time called for it
I trusted you, and you claimed you trusted me
I'm sitting here shaking my head, wondering where it all went wrong
I can't for the life of me wrap my head around it
Having a hard time figuring out where our wires got crossed
Loyalty died, and lies were told
Now we barely talk, communication waxed cold
Animosity is our new resident, taking up residency in our hearts
How could a bond so solid, grow to be so cold
We've become enemies within the same household
This blows me away
Some bonds are never meant to be broken
But ours is beyond repair

My Thoughts

He saw me, with all my attempts to avoid him
I saw him, looking good, and I know he was smelling good
We turned slightly to the right and they saw us
Everybody whose anybody, knows were an item
I mean errbody
And this is where the confusion begins
He knows I'm your woman
And you're my man
We been down for years
And some change now
That sign was blinking like neon lights
For all to see
Off limits flashes before their eyes
This is so very wrong
Cause I've been seeing him behind your back
I can't get caught displaying my feelings
If so this will end real bad so I keep them concealed
And act as though nothing is going on

You Chose

I was the unluckiest candidate
Questions roamed through my head
Wondering if I was your type
I didn't feel I made the cut, adequate
Thought you had me benched in the friend zone
You didn't give off the vibe your interest
Had changed
Mixed signals every time we came in contact
Confused is where you left me at
And to my surprise you let the cat out the bag
And shared your feelings
Insuring me they were for real
Time had revealed the secrets of your heart
You wanted me for more than a friend
That was a big deal
No longer was I in the dark
And behind my back you were making plans for our future
And you sealed the deal with a ring, and a proposal

The Dark

You had plans of keeping me in the dark

Hid it from me

The adulterous behavior

Multiple lovers

The lies

And the repeated premeditated deceit

You devised strategically to keep it hidden

You're a gangster

Using street tactics

You like playing games

Do I look like an arcade game to you

Boy get some act right, I'm about to bust your balloon

My eyes are now wide opened

You done lost a good thang

Cause I'm not going to tolerate

Your cheating, lowdown good for nothing self

The light of truth has now shined on you

And you've been exposed

I Can't Believe This

You still lying
I can't believe this
I honestly thought after you got caught
You would immediately stop
I guess not
You are prone to lie
You simply refuse to tell the truth
It just isn't in you is it
This is a crying shame
Cause nobody can trust you because of it
We question every word that comes out of your mouth
We really want to believe you
But you just like your father
A liar
We are not going to get anywhere until you are willing to tell the truth
And the whole truth
So, help you God
When you lie you get
More entangled
And the truth becomes harder and harder to find

The World As I Knew It

The year is 2020, I fell asleep one night
And woke up to a whole new world
A global pandemic had hit the world
Catching some millions off guard
There was a different feeling in the atmosphere
The world had transformed over night
I felt as though I had just stepped into the twilight zone
Someone please pinch me
I feel as though I am an actor
In one of the end time movies
Is this reality
Or some crazy demented dream
Maybe I need to go bac to sleep and wake up again
I wonder if that would make any difference
Am I witnessing the new world agenda
Unfold
Fear has cloaked mankind
Blinding their eyes with terror
We must fight, we cannot allow fear to choke
The life out of us
Remember, where there is life, there is hope

Don't Go

I am pleading and begging for you to stay
What can I do? To make you stay…
What must I say? Is, I love you, not enough?
I will be lost without you
How can you break your promises
Without any conviction
You promised me you would never leave
You gave me no warning of your departure
I never saw the signs
Thoughts race through my mind, unharnessed
Is there someone else
Or have you just falling out of love
Talk to me
Don't have me looking like a fool
I loved you deeply
The betrayal stings
What about us, our children
Are you throwing it away
Do we mean anything

Denial

No more hiding, locked in denial
Be still my heart, beating at rapid speeds
Racing uncontrollably
Palms sweaty, struggling to breath
I feel as though the life has been knocked out of me
Emotional calamity, and blurred vision
A natural disaster, I cannot believe this is happening
Wake me up
You promised me for ever
You said you loved me
Forever was not yours to give
How do you expect me to recover
I have much vested in this relationship
It's hard for me to come to the grips with
You have abandoned me time after, time
One continual heart break, after another
Left once again to pick up the pieces
Lost in denial

Put it to an End

Stop for a moment
Think about your first move
Before you make it
Reevaluate your situation
Make the right decision
Where are your choices getting you
Are you truly where you want to be in life
Or are you repeating destructive patterns
That road leads to a dead end
Its way pastime that you
Consciously, look at your life
It's time to change
For some change is uncomfortable
But necessary
Stop entangling yourself
In meaningless relationships
Put and end to bad habits
Put an end to fear
And finally muster up the strength to
Believe in yourself

Words

Words that build
Words that destroy
Words that create life
And words that speak death
Words that spoke things into existence
Words have destroyed kingdoms
Words of comfort
Words of love that make the heart glad
Words of discouragement
That breaks the spirit, and
Words of hope, that gives one strength
Words of fear, that paralyzes, restricting movement
Words of abuse, that spew from venomous tongues
And words of victory after a battle is won
Words, words, words.
There is life and death in the power of the tongue

Promises

You promised me the house with
A white picket fence, yellow trimming, and a rose garden
You promised me my dream wedding, Chantilly, and lace
You promised me a life without worries,
      you would take care of everything
You promised me it would be just you and I,
      without interference
You promised me I could trust your word,
      you told me you would never lie
You promised me a ring as big as Mt Everest,
      you would be able to see it a mile away
      all my friends would be jealous, blinded with envy
You promised me my dream car on 24's, cream and black
You promised me you would never cheat on me
      I was the only woman who had your eye, you swore it
All your promises went out the
Window the day I caught you with her
I guess you promised her the same thing

Lies

Lies that flow from serpents' tongues
Venomous entities masquerading as a friend
While they plot and plan strategically when to strike
It's no longer the knife in the back
You to must be aware of the bite
It's quick and often undetected
When they strike
Keep your eyes open
And beware
They walk among you

Us

They know nothing about us
It's funny how they attempt to define
Who we are to each other
They cleary have no idea
We've been in love for years
We just choose to leave the outside
World out of who we are
Leaving it untainted
By their views of
What they think we should be
To look at us
It would not appear to be a match made in heaven
And odd combination
And yet, we do not allow that to stop us
Without prejudices
Love is love

Come Away

Come away with me
Leave all this behind you
There is nothing here for you
But bad memories
Let me take you to a place
Where you will forget about
This place putting it all behind you
Starting fresh, with a clean slate
Creating a new chapter in your life
You can always start over; you don't have to be stuck
No matter the situation, or circumstances
You can begin again
Come away with me
To a new life
That's awaiting

The Ocean

I loved our time at the ocean
Beautiful, unforgettable memories were created
The sounds of the waves crashing against the shore
The seaguls that perched themselves in front our room door
To the birds that flew in unison at night
What a glorious sight, not leaving one behind
Fine dining, and good company
Shared love, mental ecstasy
Take me back to the ocean
So, I can get lost in the moment
Fireplaces, and good conversation
Intoxicated
The ocean
The waves
The sunset
And you
How I long to go to the ocean

View

My view may not be your view
We are individuals who see things
In a totally different light
It don't make
Us wrong
And it don't make us right
We have a right to our own opinions
Which should be respected
Not challenged, or tested
Views are based on your perception
What I see you may not
And then on the other hand
A day may come of the meeting of the minds
But until that day comes
We'll respect each other's views

Cold

You've been cold towards me lately
Is there something you're not telling me
Is there something I need to know
Something has shifted between us
And it's puzzling the heck out of me
What is going on
I can usually read your actions
I must confess, you got me confused
Hmm…
This is not like you to keep me wondering
I'm simply curious why are you so cold

Friendship

Friends are supposed to last forever
Withstanding the test of time
Weathering every storm together
The bearer of each other's secrets
Never to tell a soul
Standing by them through thick and thin
Through life they grow old
Fighting alongside the other
Every battle, engaging in war if must
A companion till the end, that's a friend
A trusted confidant when everyone else can't be trusted
A shoulder to cry on, and a shoulder to lean on
Truly a friend to the end

Attraction

There was an instant attraction
Tall dark and handsome
The very first time I saw you
I said within myself, he's fine
I was drawn to you
Like a moth to a flame, cliché
A desire grew within me to have you
All for myself, to enjoy every aspect of you
But first I needed to get more acquainted with you
To see what frequency, you were on
See if we would be able to flow
I needed to see if our vibe was equal
I wanted to know if our minds were on
The same mental plane
Or were you on that bull', you know that crap
Playing games, like you're still a child
Or were you at that point
You wanted to do something different
To get a different result
Do you want something real
Or have you decided to stick with the lames
Is my question

Belief

My belief in the creator was already there
That was not the problem, I was the problem
It's the belief in myself that I kept having an issue with
Although, I had accomplished things that brought
Recognition, it was overshadowed with fear
I still doubted in some areas
Which led me to be fearful about the next step
I wrestled with that unbelief, in the ring of self will
And made a conscious decision
After winning that fight
To go forward, run after my dreams
Like there is no tomorrow
No matter how hard it may be
I made it up in my mind, that I would
Tap into my talents, and gifts
I am allowing them to flourish
And when I did, a whole new world evolved
And they took the helm
And my life has never been the same

Prison

When you went to prison
I felt as though I let you down
I finally came to grips with, it was not my fault
Oftentimes we take on false responsibilities
Carrying baggage that don't belong to us
Feeling obligated cause that person is our loved one
We condemn ourselves for other's mistakes
While shifting the focus from them, to us
When their actions were completely out of our control
We were nowhere in the vicinity
They had all control; it was based on the choices that they made
To break the law, rebel against authority
Choosing to disobey the law of the land
Handing themselves willingly over to the judicial system
That waits patiently, to strip them from their freedom,
Whatever the driving reason they know
Who let you down
You let you down
By succumbing to the forces that be
Easy money, women, and the enticement of the game
I was carrying around a false sense of guilt
No, I know I wasn't to blame

Tell Me

Tell me what's on your heart
Don't be afraid
Let it out
You've been holding it in to long
I can handle it
I can see in your eyes it's weighing on you
Release it
Why is it taking you so long
Are you afraid by being honest
You'll lose me
Your silence
Is concerning
What is wrong
I'm here for you
Just tell me

OFF

I shook it of

Let it run off my back

Like a duck does water

I refused to let it

Tare me down

Or dampen my spirits

I will not allow another person's

Opinion of me define who I am

I took it off

The garment of people's judgement

That is, which

Did not align itself with my destiny

I decided to be me, in all my frailties

And if that wasn't acceptable so what

I shook it off the inadequacies, of the past

And I moved forward in my future

How Can You Love Us Both

When you kiss them do you think of me
Or when you kiss me do you think of them
When you touch me, do they come to mind
Or when you're in their arms
Does my face flash before your eyes
Are you stringing both of us along
Or has greed consumed you
And one person is not enough
Tell me what they lack
And what I have that draws you to me
They don't know about me
But I know about them
What an awkward place to be in
You're theirs
And mine
This is mind blowing
What a tangled web
How can you love us both?
How is your heart divided?

Retake

Can we do this over
I think we started out rocky
Let's get on the same vibe
Rewind the day
Start fresh
New page
And a clean slate
Forget about yesterday
Putting it all behind us
Let me reintroduce ourselves
Get reacquainted
Putting our differences aside
And do a retake

Climb Higher

Climb higher
Don't be afraid to chase your dreams
The world is waiting
Take your place among the stars
Don't settle for the mediocre
You were created for more
Believe in yourself
Dust off your ambition
Put to rest low-self-esteem
You can do it
It's in you
Everything you need
Climb higher
What's waiting for you
Is at the top

Tell Me Again

Tell me repeatedly
How much you love me
How I long to hear it
Serenade me with the music from your heart
I am mesmerized
Lost within its melody

Tell me again how I am
The love of your life
And you belong to me
Forever and always

Tell me again how I'm your soulmate
Never to be replaced
And no one can take my place
Tell me again we were meant to be

Courage

Be strong and of good courage

Do not be afraid

You are not alone

You don't have to face this by yourself

I will not abandon you

I'm with you all the way

You will face this, and overcome this

The obstacle will be moved out your way

The enemy you fear will not have victory over you

Be encouraged let not your heart be troubled

Neither be dismayed

I have your back

Believe it will get better

Victory is around the corner

I decree it this day

Have courage

Help is on the way

Temptation

Yield not

Unto temptation

Watch

Be cautious

Danger awaits

Discern your surroundings

Believe not every word everything look good

And good for you

Just because you can do a thing

Doesn't mean you should

Fight the urge to give in

Resist and it will flee

Temptations come to test, and try you

Will you fall or stand in the face

Of temptation

Love

I have loved you with an undying love
A love that's not based on condition kind of love
Loving you with all your imperfections and frailties
Loving you regardless of your past mistakes
And insecurities

I love you how we love each other
As I help you recover from your heartbreaks
That were caused by others
Patiently allowing you to heal
I love you with the purest love
One person could feel for another

I love you, I've waited for you all my life
You're a dream come true
I love you
You're for me, and I you

WITHIN

I looked within
And discovered I was still wounded
My heart needed healing
I was harboring the pain
Left by the last heartbreak
And I was decaying inside
I looked within, and saw my soul
Was hurt, how would I ever recover
The blow of your betrayal ran deep
Deeper than I could have ever imagined
I was hemorrhaging
I took time and did a self eval
How could this have gone undetected
Did I ignore all the warning signs
Was I so locked into you in my mind
That I became numb
And unresponsive
I looked within and reacquainted myself with me
I had become a stranger to myself
And I discovered that when I looked within

It's Not Okay

It's not okay to treat me less than a lady
It's not okay to call me out my name
It's not okay to put your hands on me violently
It's not okay to force sex upon me
It's not okay to brow beat me
It's not okay to shame me or embarrass me in front of other's
Point blank period it's not okay to disrespect me
I know my worth and value
And I'm not sticking around
'Cause your abusive treatment towards me
Is not okay

Sorry

Have you ever thought?

How many times can I say I'm sorry, to someone

And the person

Still doesn't forgive you

No matter how hard you try

To make a mend

It appears

They are trying to make you pay for what you did

Repeatedly

Without any resolve

Your only responsible of saying it once

And if they don't forgive you

You have freed yourself

Now it's on them

I'm Done

I'm done

I know I've said I was done before

Don't laugh

But now I really mean it

There is no going back

He really messed up this time

This one really broke the camel's back

I know I said that the last time

But this time I'm serious

How can you constantly leave the

Cap off the toothpaste

It's over

And that's that

I'm done

Jump

Leap

Take the risk

Don't fear

Success is waiting

Jump in with both feet

Cut the strings

That are holding you back

And jump

Jump into the unknown

There are new things to discover

A whole new world is out there

Jump

And watch the world unfold

Before your eyes

#

I can ask you why until I'm blue in the face
I wonder if you would even tell me the truth
I question some of the moves you are making
Seems really sketchy, you know
It's unlike you
And other's have noticed it to
You starting to move funny
It's out of your character
I'm uneasy around you
And we've been close since age six
Reveal your hand
Cause I ain't with this
Why all the secrecy
Why the hidden agenda
Why these new cats you are bringing around
Nobody knows
Why suddenly, the change
Why
Bro

No More

I know you have another woman
And you're lying to us both
Do you think we are fools
We've already talked
And you are dead wrong
Own up to what you've done and tell the truth
Cause I've already
Packed your clothes
I'm done with you
Go back to her if she'll have you
Cause you've burned this bridge
By the fuel of your lies
You will never cross this way again
The heart I gave you
You didn't deserve
No more will I allow
You to do this to me

River

First shock took over
Then numbness, then loss of breath
The anger that roared within me
Quaked my entire being
Instantly I was overwhelmed with grief
Rage took the helm; I was a stranger even to myself
I walked around in a daze, drowning in my emotions
How could you leave me,
How could you leave without saying goodbye
I cried a river; death took you like a thief in the night
I cried a river the day you left this earth
My world came crashing down
I attempt to rebuild the ruins
But it ain't easy
Cause missing you
Has become priority

Treason

Biblically it's not sound
You're pushing the envelope
Walking the tight rope
Challenging what's factual
Trying to make it bend to your liking
Rearranging words to fit
Your situation because you don't like his input
Cause what you want to do is not aligning with his plan
You're walking on dangerous grounds
He means what he said
And said what he means
It's not for you to agree
Honesty, right is right
You are dealing with the holy of holies
And he doesn't have to bend to your will
It's for us to surrender our will to him
To disobey his commandments is treason

Sin

The sinful nature of man, and Adam's fall
Direct or indirect rebellion is forbidden
He's speaking from his throne with power and might
By the sound of his voice the wicked run with fright
Thinking they can hide in the shadow of night
He has revealed their secret plight by his glorious light
Refusing to heed his council
And obey his laws, as sin consumes their bodies, they all fall
From the earth you hear cries of destruction, and despair
Still they refuse to repent though help is so near
Decaying and mortifying flesh
In the grave without God there's no rest
In the grave without God there's no rest
In the grave without God there's no rest
He speaks from his throne with power and might
Although it feels good to the flesh, yet damaging to the soul
Enticed by worldly pleasures until it consumes you
It has a hold on you, refusing to let you go
You are held captive
Heed his call before it's too late
He's speaking from his throne
Let him that hath an ear hear

Slowdown

You are moving completely too fast
You may miss something
Calm down and relax
Everything is going to be simply fine
Relax your mind
And unwind
Slow down your heart is racing
Quit this unnecessary pacing
And your blood pressure is elevated
What is the rush
Everything has a time limit
You cannot rush perfection
Things happen when they are supposed to
Anything forced ain't worth having
Breath
You will notice what's important when you slowdown

Puppet

I'm not your puppet, tucked away in a box
Although, you feel you're controlling my every move
Don't be deceived, you have no clue
I have a mind; I can think for myself
I will not be controlled or
Manipulated by you, or nobody else
You feast off the weak, intoxicated with their fears
The feeble-minded woman is your addiction
Luring you into her web of silliness
Anyone strong becomes a
Threat
You can't handle one on one combat
I'm not your puppet
My existence is not for your amusement

Race

Run the race

Don't give up

Complete the task

You will come out on top

If you don't faint

Victory

Is just

Around the corner

The Track

Young girls
Displayed like property
Walk hours to meet a quota
Scared, and Hungary
They can't come off the blade moneyless
Homeless, and destitute
Family ties severed
Thrown to the wolves
That prey on the
Wounded flesh
They smell blood miles away
And they are quick to run
To take advantage of
Their situation
To capitalize
On their misfortune
It all goes down on the track

ENCOUNTER

My first encounter with you

was a dream

come true

fantasy made real

Rebellion

I rebelled against everything
That went against my purpose
And my destiny
I and determined and focused

Help

Help is on the way
Hold on, don't give up
Your cries have been heard
Just wait a little while longer
Help is on the way

Voice

My voice will not be silenced
I will shout it from the roof top
I am somebody, I won't let anyone take that from me
Many have attempted to muffle my voice
And silence me because they didn't agree
But I will be heard
I will stand up for what is right
And advocate for them that don't have a
Voice, that are crying in the night
I will speak for those who struggle to be heard
Advocate for the less fortunate
My message matters
And my voice will be heard

Vision

Write it down

Make sure it's understandable

Outline the details

Leave nothing out

Make sure it's plain

So, you can see your vision manifest

In this realm

Not My Problem

That's not my problem
That does not concern me
That's they business
I'm not interested in knowing anything
Why are you so concerned with
What shouldn't concern you at all
You're that noisy neighbor
That sweeps around
Everybody's else's
Door except yours
Hmm suspect
you too involved
their problem, is not my problem
and it shouldn't be your problem either

Guilt

Guilt can eat away at you like a cancer
Eroding the soul
And polluting the mind
Sleepless nights

Regret

Regret is a secret
Enemy
That keeps
You bound to the past

Bosom

Lay your head in my bosom

Comforted by my embrace

Forget about your

Troubles

This is your safe place

Tell me the things on your mind

Unload

For the weight you are carrying is heavy

Let the tears flow

It's alright

I'm here for you

This is the night

To free yourself of that

Heaven burden

And it all begins

As you lay your head gently on my bosom

Release

Be free

Cycles

Breaking cycles
Is never easy at first
Some cycles people have been
Trapped in for years
Drugs, alcohol, and physical abuse
Just to name a few
All these cycles are detrimental
And cause lasting effects
It left unchecked
We must address
Every negative cycle in our lives
And move toward the future
It's for the betterment of self
And, so is change

Remarkable

You are remarkable
Let me say that again you
Are remarkable
Absolutely remarkable
Repeat after me
I am remarkable

Subtitles

Have you ever thought to yourself

Not out loud

But inwardly

That some people may need subtitles

When talking to you

Cause they act like

They don't understand a word you are saying

Or is it just me

Soul Searching

I have searched for you
And found you
After years of praying
Hoping and wishing
My search has finally come to an end
A heart that matches mine
A love so pure
So divine
A soul match
A one in a lifetime
Love
Rare
And priceless

Value

I know my worth
And it's not predicated
On your opinion
You don't define me
Neither do I live my life
According
To your expectations of me
liberated

Past

I put the past behind me
I buried it
Never to revisit it again
A new day has dawned
A better future has begun

Finally

Finally
We can address the elephant in the room
Has anyone noticed that her, and I
Have on the exact same outfit
Or has everyone just chosen to ignore the facts
Is it to spare my feelings
Darling
Please
I'm just as shocked
As everyone else is
How dare she desecrate
Such an elaborate garment
No don't think I'm speaking ill will of her
I'm just blown away
No honestly
Who looks better in it
Her or me

Talents

Use your talents

Don't bury them in the ground

Tap into who you are

Get connected with your purpose

And destiny

Embrace your creativity

For your talent is a part of who you are

LEAH M. KELLEY was born in Stamford, Connecticut on Dec 19th, 1969. She is the eldest of seven children. She grew up in Sacramento, California. She is an internationally published poet.

Leah received her honorary Doctorate in Divinity on October 18th, 2019. She is also a mother of six: four sons and two daughters. She is a grandmother of eleven beautiful grandchildren. Leah has been writing for forty-four years; her love of poetry grew at a young age.

Leah is also a lover of the arts, an actress, and enjoys writing praise and worship songs. She thanks God for the gifts He has bestowed upon her.

www.ingramcontent.com/pod-product-compliance
Lightning Source LLC
Chambersburg PA
CBHW070155080526
44586CB00015B/1995